TRAVEL JOURNAL

First published in 2019 by Erin Rose Publishing

Text and illustration copyright © 2019 Erin Rose Publishing

Design: Julie Anson

THIS TRAVEL JOURNAL BELONGS TO:

....

AGE: ....

TRAVEL
let's go

My Adventure To:

MY JOURNEY STARTS AT: ....

AND ENDS IN: ....

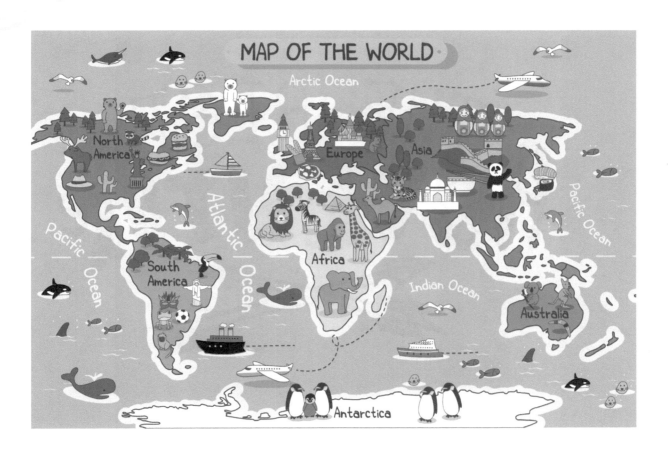

JANUARY	FEBRUARY	MARCH	APRIL	MAY	JUNE	JULY	AUGUST	SEPTEMBER	OCTOBER	NOVEMBER	DECEMBER

THE BEST ADVENTURE

HOW LONG IS THE JOURNEY? ....

HOW AM I TRAVELLING? ....

WHERE AM I STAYING? ....

WHO IS GOING? ....

WHAT WOULD I LIKE TO DO WHEN I GET THERE? ....

....

....

....

....

....

WHAT AM I MOST LOOKING FORWARD TO? ....

....

....

....

WHAT DO I NEED TO PACK? YOU CAN WRITE YOUR PACKING LIST BELOW:

....

....

....

....

....

....

....

....

....

....

....

....

DATE:................... LOCATION:....................................... TODAY'S STAR RATING: ☆ ☆ ☆ ☆ ☆

TRAVELLED BY: ✈ PLANE ☐ 🚢 BOAT ☐ 🛣 ROAD ☐ 🪧 WALK ☐ 🎈 OTHER ☐

WHERE DID I VISIT?

WHO WAS THERE?

WHAT I DISCOVERED?

WHO DID I MEET?

MY FAVOURITE THING WAS:

MY MOOD WAS 😄 ☐ 🙂 ☐ 😐 ☐ 🙁 ☐ 😎 ☐ 😴 ☐

WEATHER ☀ ☐ ⛅ ☐ 🌥 ☐ ⛈ ☐ 🌧 ☐ 🌨 ☐

PICTURE OF THE DAY

DRAW, SKETCH OR STICK-IN A PICTURE OR KEEPSAKE OF YOUR DAY.

DATE:........................ LOCATION: .... TODAY'S STAR RATING: ☆ ☆ ☆ ☆ ☆

TRAVELLED BY: ✈ ☐ 🚢 ☐ 🛣 ☐ 🪧 ☐ 🎈 ☐
PLANE   BOAT   ROAD   WALK   OTHER

WHERE DID I VISIT?

WHO WAS THERE?

WHAT I DISCOVERED?

WHO DID I MEET?

MY FAVOURITE THING WAS:

MY MOOD WAS 😄 ☐ 🙂 ☐ 😐 ☐ 🙁 ☐ 😎 ☐ 😴 ☐

WEATHER ☀ ☐ ⛅ ☐ 🌦 ☐ ⛈ ☐ 🌧 ☐ 🌨 ☐

PICTURE OF THE DAY

DRAW, SKETCH OR STICK-IN A PICTURE OR KEEPSAKE OF YOUR DAY.

DATE:........................ LOCATION:.. TODAY'S STAR RATING: ☆ ☆ ☆ ☆ ☆

TRAVELLED BY: ✈ ☐ 🚢 ☐ 🛣 ☐ 🪧 ☐ 🎈 ☐
PLANE   BOAT   ROAD   WALK   OTHER

WHERE DID I VISIT?

WHO WAS THERE?

WHAT I DISCOVERED?

WHO DID I MEET?

MY FAVOURITE THING WAS:

MY MOOD WAS 😄 ☐ 🙂 ☐ 😐 ☐ 🙁 ☐ 😎 ☐ 😴 ☐

WEATHER ☀ ☐ ⛅ ☐ 🌦 ☐ ⛈ ☐ 🌧 ☐ 🌨 ☐

PICTURE OF THE DAY

DRAW, SKETCH OR STICK-IN A PICTURE OR KEEPSAKE OF YOUR DAY.

DATE:......................... LOCATION:..................................... TODAY'S STAR RATING: ☆☆☆☆☆

TRAVELLED BY: ✈ ☐ 🚢 ☐ 🛣 ☐ 🚏 ☐ 🎈 ☐
PLANE   BOAT   ROAD   WALK   OTHER

WHERE DID I VISIT?

WHO WAS THERE?

WHAT I DISCOVERED?

WHO DID I MEET?

MY FAVOURITE THING WAS:

MY MOOD WAS 😄 ☐ 🙂 ☐ 😐 ☐ ☹ ☐ 😎 ☐ 😴 ☐

WEATHER ☀ ☐ ⛅ ☐ 🌦 ☐ ⛈ ☐ 🌧 ☐ 🌨 ☐

PICTURE OF THE DAY

DRAW, SKETCH OR STICK-IN A PICTURE OR KEEPSAKE OF YOUR DAY.

DATE:...................... LOCATION:.. TODAY'S STAR RATING: ☆ ☆ ☆ ☆ ☆

TRAVELLED BY: ✈ PLANE ☐   🚢 BOAT ☐   🚗 ROAD ☐   🪧 WALK ☐   🎈 OTHER ☐

WHERE DID I VISIT?

WHO WAS THERE?

WHAT I DISCOVERED?

WHO DID I MEET?

MY FAVOURITE THING WAS:

MY MOOD WAS   😄 ☐   🙂 ☐   😐 ☐   🙁 ☐   😎 ☐   😴 ☐

WEATHER   ☀ ☐   ⛅ ☐   🌦 ☐   ⛈ ☐   🌧 ☐   🌨 ☐

PICTURE OF THE DAY

DRAW, SKETCH OR STICK-IN A PICTURE OR KEEPSAKE OF YOUR DAY.

DATE:........................ LOCATION:... TODAY'S STAR RATING: ☆ ☆ ☆ ☆ ☆

TRAVELLED BY: ✈ PLANE ☐ 🚢 BOAT ☐ 🛣 ROAD ☐ 🪧 WALK ☐ 🎈 OTHER ☐

WHERE DID I VISIT?

WHO WAS THERE?

WHAT I DISCOVERED?

WHO DID I MEET?

MY FAVOURITE THING WAS:

MY MOOD WAS 😄 ☐ 🙂 ☐ 😐 ☐ ☹ ☐ 😎 ☐ 😴 ☐

WEATHER ☀ ☐ ⛅ ☐ 🌦 ☐ ⛈ ☐ 🌧 ☐ 🌨 ☐

PICTURE OF THE DAY

DRAW, SKETCH OR STICK-IN A PICTURE OR KEEPSAKE OF YOUR DAY.

DATE:........................ LOCATION: .... TODAY'S STAR RATING: ☆ ☆ ☆ ☆ ☆

TRAVELLED BY: PLANE ☐ BOAT ☐ ROAD ☐ WALK ☐ OTHER ☐

WHERE DID I VISIT?

WHO WAS THERE?

WHAT I DISCOVERED?

WHO DID I MEET?

MY FAVOURITE THING WAS:

MY MOOD WAS 😄 ☐ 🙂 ☐ 😐 ☐ 🙁 ☐ 😎 ☐ 😴 ☐

WEATHER ☐ ☐ ☐ ☐ ☐ ☐

PICTURE OF THE DAY

DRAW, SKETCH OR STICK-IN A PICTURE OR KEEPSAKE OF YOUR DAY.

DATE:................ LOCATION:... TODAY'S STAR RATING: ☆☆☆☆☆

TRAVELLED BY: ✈ ☐ 🚢 ☐ 🛣 ☐ 🪧 ☐ 🎈 ☐
PLANE   BOAT   ROAD   WALK   OTHER

WHERE DID I VISIT?

WHO WAS THERE?

WHAT I DISCOVERED?

WHO DID I MEET?

MY FAVOURITE THING WAS:

MY MOOD WAS 😄 ☐ 🙂 ☐ 😐 ☐ 🙁 ☐ 😎 ☐ 😴 ☐

WEATHER ☀ ☐ ⛅ ☐ 🌦 ☐ ⛈ ☐ 🌧 ☐ 🌨 ☐

PICTURE OF THE DAY

DRAW, SKETCH OR STICK-IN A PICTURE OR KEEPSAKE OF YOUR DAY.

DATE:........................ LOCATION:... TODAY'S STAR RATING: ☆ ☆ ☆ ☆ ☆

TRAVELLED BY: ✈ ☐ 🚢 ☐ 🚗 ☐ 🪧 ☐ 🎈 ☐
PLANE   BOAT   ROAD   WALK   OTHER

WHERE DID I VISIT?

WHO WAS THERE?

WHAT I DISCOVERED?

WHO DID I MEET?

MY FAVOURITE THING WAS:

MY MOOD WAS 😄 ☐ 🙂 ☐ 😐 ☐ 🙁 ☐ 😎 ☐ 😴 ☐

WEATHER ☀ ☐ ⛅ ☐ 🌦 ☐ ⛈ ☐ 🌧 ☐ 🌨 ☐

PICTURE OF THE DAY

DRAW, SKETCH OR STICK-IN A PICTURE OR KEEPSAKE OF YOUR DAY.

DATE:........................ LOCATION:.. TODAY'S STAR RATING: ☆ ☆ ☆ ☆ ☆

TRAVELLED BY: ✈ ☐ 🚢 ☐ 🛣 ☐ 🪧 ☐ 🎈 ☐
PLANE   BOAT   ROAD   WALK   OTHER

WHERE DID I VISIT?

WHO WAS THERE?

WHAT I DISCOVERED?

WHO DID I MEET?

MY FAVOURITE THING WAS:

MY MOOD WAS 😄 ☐ 🙂 ☐ 😐 ☐ 🙁 ☐ 😎 ☐ 😴 ☐

WEATHER ☀ ☐ ⛅ ☐ 🌥 ☐ ⛈ ☐ 🌧 ☐ 🌨 ☐

PICTURE OF THE DAY

DRAW, SKETCH OR STICK-IN A PICTURE OR KEEPSAKE OF YOUR DAY.

DATE:...................... LOCATION: .... TODAY'S STAR RATING: ☆ ☆ ☆ ☆ ☆

TRAVELLED BY: ☐ PLANE ☐ BOAT ☐ ROAD ☐ WALK ☐ OTHER

WHERE DID I VISIT?

WHO WAS THERE?

WHAT I DISCOVERED?

WHO DID I MEET?

MY FAVOURITE THING WAS:

MY MOOD WAS 😆 ☐ 🙂 ☐ 😐 ☐ ☹️ ☐ 😎 ☐ 😴 ☐

WEATHER ☀️ ☐ ⛅ ☐ 🌦️ ☐ ⛈️ ☐ 🌧️ ☐ 🌨️ ☐

PICTURE OF THE DAY

DRAW, SKETCH OR STICK-IN A PICTURE OR KEEPSAKE OF YOUR DAY.

DATE:........................ LOCATION:.. TODAY'S STAR RATING: ☆☆☆☆☆

TRAVELLED BY: ✈ ☐ 🚢 ☐ 🛣 ☐ 🪧 ☐ 🎈 ☐
PLANE   BOAT   ROAD   WALK   OTHER

WHERE DID I VISIT?

WHO WAS THERE?

WHAT I DISCOVERED?

WHO DID I MEET?

MY FAVOURITE THING WAS:

MY MOOD WAS 😄 ☐ 🙂 ☐ 😐 ☐ 🙁 ☐ 😎 ☐ 😴 ☐

WEATHER ☀ ☐ ⛅ ☐ 🌦 ☐ ⛈ ☐ 🌧 ☐ 🌨 ☐

PICTURE OF THE DAY

DRAW, SKETCH OR STICK-IN A PICTURE OR KEEPSAKE OF YOUR DAY.

DATE:...................... LOCATION:.. TODAY'S STAR RATING: ☆☆☆☆☆

TRAVELLED BY: ✈ PLANE ☐   🚢 BOAT ☐   🛣 ROAD ☐   🪧 WALK ☐   🎈 OTHER ☐

WHERE DID I VISIT?

WHO WAS THERE?

WHAT I DISCOVERED?

WHO DID I MEET?

MY FAVOURITE THING WAS:

MY MOOD WAS 😄 ☐ 🙂 ☐ 😐 ☐ ☹ ☐ 😎 ☐ 😴 ☐

WEATHER ☀ ☐ ⛅ ☐ 🌦 ☐ ⛈ ☐ 🌧 ☐ 🌨 ☐

PICTURE OF THE DAY

DRAW, SKETCH OR STICK-IN A PICTURE OR KEEPSAKE OF YOUR DAY.

DATE:...................... LOCATION:.. TODAY'S STAR RATING: ☆ ☆ ☆ ☆ ☆

TRAVELLED BY: ✈ ☐ 🚢 ☐ 🛣 ☐ 🪧 ☐ 🎈 ☐
PLANE   BOAT   ROAD   WALK   OTHER

WHERE DID I VISIT?

WHO WAS THERE?

WHAT I DISCOVERED?

WHO DID I MEET?

MY FAVOURITE THING WAS:

MY MOOD WAS 😄 ☐ 🙂 ☐ 😐 ☐ 🙁 ☐ 😎 ☐ 😴 ☐

WEATHER ☀ ☐ ⛅ ☐ 🌥 ☐ ⛈ ☐ 🌧 ☐ ❄ ☐

PICTURE OF THE DAY

DRAW, SKETCH OR STICK-IN A PICTURE OR KEEPSAKE OF YOUR DAY.

DATE:........................ LOCATION: .... TODAY'S STAR RATING: ☆ ☆ ☆ ☆ ☆

TRAVELLED BY: ✈ ☐   🚢 ☐   🛣 ☐   🪧 ☐   🎈 ☐
PLANE   BOAT   ROAD   WALK   OTHER

WHERE DID I VISIT?

WHO WAS THERE?

WHAT I DISCOVERED?

WHO DID I MEET?

MY FAVOURITE THING WAS:

MY MOOD WAS   😄 ☐   🙂 ☐   😐 ☐   🙁 ☐   😎 ☐   😴 ☐

WEATHER   ☀ ☐   ⛅ ☐   🌦 ☐   ⛈ ☐   🌧 ☐   🌨 ☐

PICTURE OF THE DAY

DRAW, SKETCH OR STICK-IN A PICTURE OR KEEPSAKE OF YOUR DAY.

DATE:........................ LOCATION: .... TODAY'S STAR RATING: ☆ ☆ ☆ ☆ ☆

TRAVELLED BY: ✈ ☐ 🚢 ☐ 🛣 ☐ 🪧 ☐ 🎈 ☐
PLANE   BOAT   ROAD   WALK   OTHER

WHERE DID I VISIT?

WHO WAS THERE?

WHAT I DISCOVERED?

WHO DID I MEET?

MY FAVOURITE THING WAS:

MY MOOD WAS 😄 ☐ 🙂 ☐ 😐 ☐ 🙁 ☐ 😎 ☐ 😴 ☐

WEATHER ☀ ☐ ⛅ ☐ 🌦 ☐ ⛈ ☐ 🌧 ☐ 🌨 ☐

PICTURE OF THE DAY

DRAW, SKETCH OR STICK-IN A PICTURE OR KEEPSAKE OF YOUR DAY.

DATE:........................ LOCATION: .... TODAY'S STAR RATING: ☆ ☆ ☆ ☆ ☆

TRAVELLED BY: ✈ ☐ 🚢 ☐ 🛣 ☐ 🪧 ☐ 🎈 ☐
PLANE · BOAT · ROAD · WALK · OTHER

WHERE DID I VISIT?

WHO WAS THERE?

WHAT I DISCOVERED?

WHO DID I MEET?

MY FAVOURITE THING WAS:

MY MOOD WAS 😆 ☐ 🙂 ☐ 😐 ☐ 🙁 ☐ 😎 ☐ 😴 ☐

WEATHER ☀ ☐ ⛅ ☐ 🌦 ☐ ⛈ ☐ 🌧 ☐ 🌨 ☐

PICTURE OF THE DAY

DRAW, SKETCH OR STICK-IN A PICTURE OR KEEPSAKE OF YOUR DAY.

DATE:........................ LOCATION:.. TODAY'S STAR RATING: ☆ ☆ ☆ ☆ ☆

TRAVELLED BY: ✈ ☐ 🚢 ☐ 🛣 ☐ 🚶 ☐ 🎈 ☐
               PLANE   BOAT   ROAD   WALK   OTHER

WHERE DID I VISIT?

WHO WAS THERE?

WHAT I DISCOVERED?

WHO DID I MEET?

MY FAVOURITE THING WAS:

MY MOOD WAS 😄 ☐ 🙂 ☐ 😐 ☐ 🙁 ☐ 😎 ☐ 😴 ☐

WEATHER ☀ ☐ ⛅ ☐ 🌦 ☐ ⛈ ☐ 🌧 ☐ 🌨 ☐

PICTURE OF THE DAY

DRAW, SKETCH OR STICK-IN A PICTURE OR KEEPSAKE OF YOUR DAY.

DATE:........................ LOCATION:.. TODAY'S STAR RATING: ☆ ☆ ☆ ☆ ☆

TRAVELLED BY: ✈ ☐ PLANE 🚢 ☐ BOAT 🛤 ☐ ROAD 🪧 ☐ WALK 🎈 ☐ OTHER

WHERE DID I VISIT?

WHO WAS THERE?

WHAT I DISCOVERED?

WHO DID I MEET?

MY FAVOURITE THING WAS:

MY MOOD WAS 😄 ☐ 🙂 ☐ 😐 ☐ 🙁 ☐ 😎 ☐ 😴 ☐

WEATHER ☀ ☐ ⛅ ☐ 🌦 ☐ ⛈ ☐ 🌧 ☐ 🌨 ☐

PICTURE OF THE DAY

DRAW, SKETCH OR STICK-IN A PICTURE OR KEEPSAKE OF YOUR DAY.

DATE:........................ LOCATION:.. TODAY'S STAR RATING: ☆ ☆ ☆ ☆ ☆

TRAVELLED BY: ✈ ☐ 🚢 ☐ 🛣 ☐ 🪧 ☐ 🎈 ☐
PLANE   BOAT   ROAD   WALK   OTHER

WHERE DID I VISIT?

WHO WAS THERE?

WHAT I DISCOVERED?

WHO DID I MEET?

MY FAVOURITE THING WAS:

MY MOOD WAS 😁 ☐ 🙂 ☐ 😐 ☐ 🙁 ☐ 😎 ☐ 😴 ☐

WEATHER ☀ ☐ ⛅ ☐ 🌦 ☐ ⛈ ☐ 🌧 ☐ 🌨 ☐

PICTURE OF THE DAY

DRAW, SKETCH OR STICK-IN A PICTURE OR KEEPSAKE OF YOUR DAY.

DATE:........................ LOCATION:.. TODAY'S STAR RATING: ☆ ☆ ☆ ☆ ☆

TRAVELLED BY: ✈ PLANE ☐   🚢 BOAT ☐   🛣 ROAD ☐   🪧 WALK ☐   🎈 OTHER ☐

WHERE DID I VISIT?

WHO WAS THERE?

WHAT I DISCOVERED?

WHO DID I MEET?

MY FAVOURITE THING WAS:

MY MOOD WAS 😄 ☐ 🙂 ☐ 😐 ☐ ☹ ☐ 😎 ☐ 😴 ☐

WEATHER ☀ ☐ ⛅ ☐ 🌦 ☐ ⛈ ☐ 🌧 ☐ 🌨 ☐

PICTURE OF THE DAY

DRAW, SKETCH OR STICK-IN A PICTURE OR KEEPSAKE OF YOUR DAY.

DATE:..................... LOCATION:... TODAY'S STAR RATING: ☆☆☆☆☆

TRAVELLED BY:

PLANE ☐   BOAT ☐   ROAD ☐   WALK ☐   OTHER ☐

WHERE DID I VISIT?

WHO WAS THERE?

WHAT I DISCOVERED?

WHO DID I MEET?

MY FAVOURITE THING WAS:

MY MOOD WAS 😆☐ 🙂☐ 😐☐ 🙁☐ 😎☐ 😴☐

WEATHER ☀️☐ ⛅☐ 🌥️☐ ⛈️☐ 🌧️☐ 🌨️☐

PICTURE OF THE DAY

DRAW, SKETCH OR STICK-IN A PICTURE OR KEEPSAKE OF YOUR DAY.

DATE:........................ LOCATION:... TODAY'S STAR RATING: ☆ ☆ ☆ ☆ ☆

TRAVELLED BY: ✈ PLANE ☐ 🚢 BOAT ☐ 🛣 ROAD ☐ 🪧 WALK ☐ 🎈 OTHER ☐

WHERE DID I VISIT?

WHO WAS THERE?

WHAT I DISCOVERED?

WHO DID I MEET?

MY FAVOURITE THING WAS:

MY MOOD WAS 😄 ☐ 🙂 ☐ 😐 ☐ 🙁 ☐ 😎 ☐ 😴 ☐

WEATHER ☀ ☐ ⛅ ☐ 🌦 ☐ ⛈ ☐ 🌧 ☐ 🌨 ☐

PICTURE OF THE DAY

DRAW, SKETCH OR STICK-IN A PICTURE OR KEEPSAKE OF YOUR DAY.

DATE:.................... LOCATION:... TODAY'S STAR RATING: ☆ ☆ ☆ ☆ ☆

TRAVELLED BY: ✈ ☐ 🚢 ☐ 🛣 ☐ 🪧 ☐ 🎈 ☐
PLANE   BOAT   ROAD   WALK   OTHER

WHERE DID I VISIT?

WHO WAS THERE?

WHAT I DISCOVERED?

WHO DID I MEET?

MY FAVOURITE THING WAS:

MY MOOD WAS 😄 ☐ 🙂 ☐ 😐 ☐ 🙁 ☐ 😎 ☐ 😴 ☐

WEATHER ☀ ☐ ⛅ ☐ 🌦 ☐ ⛈ ☐ 🌧 ☐ 🌨 ☐

PICTURE OF THE DAY

DRAW, SKETCH OR STICK-IN A PICTURE OR KEEPSAKE OF YOUR DAY.

DATE:........................ LOCATION: .... TODAY'S STAR RATING: ☆ ☆ ☆ ☆ ☆

TRAVELLED BY: ✈ ☐ 🚢 ☐ 🛤 ☐ 🪧 ☐ 🎈 ☐
PLANE   BOAT   ROAD   WALK   OTHER

WHERE DID I VISIT?

WHO WAS THERE?

WHAT I DISCOVERED?

WHO DID I MEET?

MY FAVOURITE THING WAS:

MY MOOD WAS 😄 ☐ 🙂 ☐ 😐 ☐ 🙁 ☐ 😎 ☐ 😴 ☐

WEATHER ☀ ☐ ⛅ ☐ 🌦 ☐ ⛈ ☐ 🌧 ☐ 🌨 ☐

PICTURE OF THE DAY

DRAW, SKETCH OR STICK-IN A PICTURE OR KEEPSAKE OF YOUR DAY.

DATE:......................... LOCATION:...................................... TODAY'S STAR RATING: ☆ ☆ ☆ ☆ ☆

TRAVELLED BY: 🛩 ☐ 🚢 ☐ 🌲 ☐ 🪧 ☐ 🎈 ☐
              PLANE   BOAT   ROAD   WALK   OTHER

WHERE DID I VISIT?

WHO WAS THERE?

WHAT I DISCOVERED?

WHO DID I MEET?

MY FAVOURITE THING WAS:

MY MOOD WAS 😄 ☐ 🙂 ☐ 😐 ☐ 🙁 ☐ 😎 ☐ 😴 ☐

WEATHER ☀ ☐ ⛅ ☐ 🌦 ☐ ⛈ ☐ 🌧 ☐ 🌨 ☐

PICTURE OF THE DAY

DRAW, SKETCH OR STICK-IN A PICTURE OR KEEPSAKE OF YOUR DAY.

DATE:........................ LOCATION:... TODAY'S STAR RATING: ☆ ☆ ☆ ☆ ☆

TRAVELLED BY: ✈ ☐ 🚢 ☐ 🛣 ☐ 🪧 ☐ 🎈 ☐
PLANE   BOAT   ROAD   WALK   OTHER

WHERE DID I VISIT?

WHO WAS THERE?

WHAT I DISCOVERED?

WHO DID I MEET?

MY FAVOURITE THING WAS:

MY MOOD WAS 😄 ☐ 🙂 ☐ 😐 ☐ 🙁 ☐ 😎 ☐ 😴 ☐

WEATHER ☀ ☐ ⛅ ☐ 🌦 ☐ ⛈ ☐ 🌧 ☐ 🌨 ☐

PICTURE OF THE DAY

DRAW, SKETCH OR STICK-IN A PICTURE OR KEEPSAKE OF YOUR DAY.

DATE:........................ LOCATION:... TODAY'S STAR RATING: ☆ ☆ ☆ ☆ ☆

TRAVELLED BY: ✈ ☐ 🚢 ☐ 🛣 ☐ 🪧 ☐ 🎈 ☐
PLANE   BOAT   ROAD   WALK   OTHER

WHERE DID I VISIT?

WHO WAS THERE?

WHAT I DISCOVERED?

WHO DID I MEET?

MY FAVOURITE THING WAS:

MY MOOD WAS 😄 ☐ 🙂 ☐ 😐 ☐ ☹ ☐ 😎 ☐ 😴 ☐

WEATHER ☀ ☐ ⛅ ☐ 🌦 ☐ ⛈ ☐ 🌧 ☐ 🌨 ☐

PICTURE OF THE DAY

DRAW, SKETCH OR STICK-IN A PICTURE OR KEEPSAKE OF YOUR DAY.

DATE:........................ LOCATION:... TODAY'S STAR RATING: ☆ ☆ ☆ ☆ ☆

TRAVELLED BY: ✈ ☐ PLANE   🚢 ☐ BOAT   🛣 ☐ ROAD   🪧 ☐ WALK   🎈 ☐ OTHER

WHERE DID I VISIT?

WHO WAS THERE?

WHAT I DISCOVERED?

WHO DID I MEET?

MY FAVOURITE THING WAS:

MY MOOD WAS 😆 ☐ 🙂 ☐ 😐 ☐ 🙁 ☐ 😎 ☐ 😴 ☐

WEATHER ☀ ☐ ⛅ ☐ 🌦 ☐ ⛈ ☐ 🌧 ☐ 🌨 ☐

PICTURE OF THE DAY

DRAW, SKETCH OR STICK-IN A PICTURE OR KEEPSAKE OF YOUR DAY.

DATE:........................ LOCATION:.. TODAY'S STAR RATING: ☆ ☆ ☆ ☆ ☆

TRAVELLED BY: ✈ □ 🚢 □ 🛣 □ 🪧 □ 🎈 □
PLANE   BOAT   ROAD   WALK   OTHER

WHERE DID I VISIT?

WHO WAS THERE?

WHAT I DISCOVERED?

WHO DID I MEET?

MY FAVOURITE THING WAS:

MY MOOD WAS 😄 □ 🙂 □ 😐 □ 🙁 □ 😎 □ 😴 □

WEATHER ☀ □ ⛅ □ 🌦 □ ⛈ □ 🌧 □ 🌨 □

PICTURE OF THE DAY

DRAW, SKETCH OR STICK-IN A PICTURE OR KEEPSAKE OF YOUR DAY.

DATE:....................... LOCATION:....................................... TODAY'S STAR RATING: ☆ ☆ ☆ ☆ ☆

TRAVELLED BY: ✈ ☐ 🚢 ☐ 🛤 ☐ 🪧 ☐ 🎈 ☐
PLANE   BOAT   ROAD   WALK   OTHER

WHERE DID I VISIT?

WHO WAS THERE?

WHAT I DISCOVERED?

WHO DID I MEET?

MY FAVOURITE THING WAS:

MY MOOD WAS   😄 ☐   🙂 ☐   😐 ☐   ☹ ☐   😎 ☐   😴 ☐

WEATHER   ☀ ☐   ⛅ ☐   🌦 ☐   ⛈ ☐   🌧 ☐   🌨 ☐

PICTURE OF THE DAY

DRAW, SKETCH OR STICK-IN A PICTURE OR KEEPSAKE OF YOUR DAY.

DATE:......................... LOCATION:... TODAY'S STAR RATING: ☆ ☆ ☆ ☆ ☆

TRAVELLED BY: ✈ □ PLANE 🚢 □ BOAT 🌪 □ ROAD 🪧 □ WALK 🎈 □ OTHER

WHERE DID I VISIT?

WHO WAS THERE?

WHAT I DISCOVERED?

WHO DID I MEET?

MY FAVOURITE THING WAS:

MY MOOD WAS 😄 □ 🙂 □ 😐 □ 🙁 □ 😎 □ 😴 □

WEATHER ☀ □ ⛅ □ 🌥 □ ⛈ □ 🌧 □ 🌨 □

PICTURE OF THE DAY

DRAW, SKETCH OR STICK-IN A PICTURE OR KEEPSAKE OF YOUR DAY.

DATE:........................ LOCATION:... TODAY'S STAR RATING: ☆ ☆ ☆ ☆ ☆

TRAVELLED BY: ✈ PLANE ☐ 🚢 BOAT ☐ 🛣 ROAD ☐ 🪧 WALK ☐ 🎈 OTHER ☐

WHERE DID I VISIT?

WHO WAS THERE?

WHAT I DISCOVERED?

WHO DID I MEET?

MY FAVOURITE THING WAS:

MY MOOD WAS 😄 ☐ 🙂 ☐ 😐 ☐ 🙁 ☐ 😎 ☐ 😴 ☐

WEATHER ☀ ☐ ⛅ ☐ 🌥 ☐ ⛈ ☐ 🌧 ☐ 🌨 ☐

PICTURE OF THE DAY

DRAW, SKETCH OR STICK-IN A PICTURE OR KEEPSAKE OF YOUR DAY.

DATE:......................... LOCATION:... TODAY'S STAR RATING: ☆ ☆ ☆ ☆ ☆

TRAVELLED BY: ✈ PLANE ☐ 🚢 BOAT ☐ 🛣 ROAD ☐ 🪧 WALK ☐ 🎈 OTHER ☐

WHERE DID I VISIT?

WHO WAS THERE?

WHAT I DISCOVERED?

WHO DID I MEET?

MY FAVOURITE THING WAS:

MY MOOD WAS 😄 ☐ 🙂 ☐ 😐 ☐ 🙁 ☐ 😎 ☐ 😴 ☐

WEATHER ☀ ☐ ⛅ ☐ 🌦 ☐ ⛈ ☐ 🌧 ☐ ❄ ☐

PICTURE OF THE DAY

DRAW, SKETCH OR STICK-IN A PICTURE OR KEEPSAKE OF YOUR DAY.

DATE:........................ LOCATION:... TODAY'S STAR RATING: ☆☆☆☆☆

TRAVELLED BY: ✈ ☐ 🚢 ☐ 🛣 ☐ 🪧 ☐ 🎈 ☐
PLANE   BOAT   ROAD   WALK   OTHER

WHERE DID I VISIT?

WHO WAS THERE?

WHAT I DISCOVERED?

WHO DID I MEET?

MY FAVOURITE THING WAS:

MY MOOD WAS 😄 ☐ 🙂 ☐ 😐 ☐ 🙁 ☐ 😎 ☐ 😴 ☐

WEATHER ☀ ☐ ⛅ ☐ 🌦 ☐ ⛈ ☐ 🌧 ☐ 🌨 ☐

PICTURE OF THE DAY

DRAW, SKETCH OR STICK-IN A PICTURE OR KEEPSAKE OF YOUR DAY.

DATE:.................... LOCATION:............................... TODAY'S STAR RATING: ☆ ☆ ☆ ☆ ☆

TRAVELLED BY: ✈ ☐ 🚢 ☐ 🛣 ☐ 🪧 ☐ 🎈 ☐
PLANE   BOAT   ROAD   WALK   OTHER

WHERE DID I VISIT?

WHO WAS THERE?

WHAT I DISCOVERED?

WHO DID I MEET?

MY FAVOURITE THING WAS:

MY MOOD WAS 😄 ☐ 🙂 ☐ 😐 ☐ 🙁 ☐ 😎 ☐ 😴 ☐

WEATHER ☀ ☐ ⛅ ☐ 🌦 ☐ ⛈ ☐ 🌧 ☐ 🌨 ☐

PICTURE OF THE DAY

DRAW, SKETCH OR STICK-IN A PICTURE OR KEEPSAKE OF YOUR DAY.

DATE:........................ LOCATION:.. TODAY'S STAR RATING: ☆ ☆ ☆ ☆ ☆

TRAVELLED BY: ✈ PLANE ☐ 🚢 BOAT ☐ 🛣 ROAD ☐ 🚏 WALK ☐ 🎈 OTHER ☐

WHERE DID I VISIT?

WHO WAS THERE?

WHAT I DISCOVERED?

WHO DID I MEET?

MY FAVOURITE THING WAS:

MY MOOD WAS 😄 ☐ 🙂 ☐ 😐 ☐ 🙁 ☐ 😎 ☐ 😴 ☐

WEATHER ☀ ☐ ⛅ ☐ 🌥 ☐ ⛈ ☐ 🌧 ☐ 🌨 ☐

PICTURE OF THE DAY

DRAW, SKETCH OR STICK-IN A PICTURE OR KEEPSAKE OF YOUR DAY.

DATE: .... LOCATION: .... TODAY'S STAR RATING: ☆ ☆ ☆ ☆ ☆

TRAVELLED BY: ✈ ☐ 🚢 ☐ 🛣 ☐ 🪧 ☐ 🎈 ☐
PLANE   BOAT   ROAD   WALK   OTHER

WHERE DID I VISIT?

WHO WAS THERE?

WHAT I DISCOVERED?

WHO DID I MEET?

MY FAVOURITE THING WAS:

MY MOOD WAS 😄 ☐ 🙂 ☐ 😐 ☐ 🙁 ☐ 😎 ☐ 😴 ☐

WEATHER ☀ ☐ ⛅ ☐ 🌦 ☐ ⛈ ☐ 🌧 ☐ 🌨 ☐

PICTURE OF THE DAY

DRAW, SKETCH OR STICK-IN A PICTURE OR KEEPSAKE OF YOUR DAY.

DATE:......................... LOCATION:... TODAY'S STAR RATING: ☆ ☆ ☆ ☆ ☆

TRAVELLED BY: ✈ □ 🚢 □ 🛣 □ 🪧 □ 🎈 □
PLANE   BOAT   ROAD   WALK   OTHER

WHERE DID I VISIT?

WHO WAS THERE?

WHAT I DISCOVERED?

WHO DID I MEET?

MY FAVOURITE THING WAS:

MY MOOD WAS 😄 □ 🙂 □ 😐 □ 🙁 □ 😎 □ 😴 □

WEATHER ☀ □ ⛅ □ 🌥 □ ⛈ □ 🌧 □ 🌨 □

PICTURE OF THE DAY

DRAW, SKETCH OR STICK-IN A PICTURE OR KEEPSAKE OF YOUR DAY.

DATE:........................ LOCATION:... TODAY'S STAR RATING: ☆ ☆ ☆ ☆ ☆

TRAVELLED BY: ✈ ☐ 🚢 ☐ 🛣 ☐ 🪧 ☐ 🎈 ☐
PLANE   BOAT   ROAD   WALK   OTHER

WHERE DID I VISIT?

WHO WAS THERE?

WHAT I DISCOVERED?

WHO DID I MEET?

MY FAVOURITE THING WAS:

MY MOOD WAS 😄 ☐ 🙂 ☐ 😐 ☐ 🙁 ☐ 😎 ☐ 😴 ☐

WEATHER ☀ ☐ ⛅ ☐ 🌦 ☐ ⛈ ☐ 🌧 ☐ 🌨 ☐

PICTURE OF THE DAY

DRAW, SKETCH OR STICK-IN A PICTURE OR KEEPSAKE OF YOUR DAY.

DATE:...................... LOCATION: .... TODAY'S STAR RATING: ☆☆☆☆☆

TRAVELLED BY: ✈ PLANE ☐ 🚢 BOAT ☐ 🛤 ROAD ☐ 🪧 WALK ☐ 🎈 OTHER ☐

WHERE DID I VISIT?

WHO WAS THERE?

WHAT I DISCOVERED?

WHO DID I MEET?

MY FAVOURITE THING WAS:

MY MOOD WAS 😆 ☐ 🙂 ☐ 😐 ☐ 🙁 ☐ 😎 ☐ 😴 ☐

WEATHER ☀ ☐ ⛅ ☐ 🌦 ☐ ⛈ ☐ 🌧 ☐ 🌨 ☐

PICTURE OF THE DAY

DRAW, SKETCH OR STICK-IN A PICTURE OR KEEPSAKE OF YOUR DAY.

DATE:........................ LOCATION: .... TODAY'S STAR RATING: ☆ ☆ ☆ ☆ ☆

TRAVELLED BY: ✈ ☐   🚢 ☐   🛣 ☐   🪧 ☐   🎈 ☐
             PLANE   BOAT   ROAD   WALK   OTHER

WHERE DID I VISIT?

WHO WAS THERE?

WHAT I DISCOVERED?

WHO DID I MEET?

MY FAVOURITE THING WAS:

MY MOOD WAS 😄 ☐ 🙂 ☐ 😐 ☐ 🙁 ☐ 😎 ☐ 😴 ☐

WEATHER ☀ ☐ ⛅ ☐ 🌦 ☐ ⛈ ☐ 🌧 ☐ 🌨 ☐

PICTURE OF THE DAY

DRAW, SKETCH OR STICK-IN A PICTURE OR KEEPSAKE OF YOUR DAY.

DATE:........................ LOCATION:.. TODAY'S STAR RATING: ☆ ☆ ☆ ☆ ☆

TRAVELLED BY: ✈ PLANE ☐ 🛳 BOAT ☐ 🛣 ROAD ☐ 🪧 WALK ☐ 🎈 OTHER ☐

WHERE DID I VISIT?

WHO WAS THERE?

WHAT I DISCOVERED?

WHO DID I MEET?

MY FAVOURITE THING WAS:

MY MOOD WAS 😄 ☐ 🙂 ☐ 😐 ☐ 🙁 ☐ 😎 ☐ 😴 ☐

WEATHER ☀ ☐ ⛅ ☐ 🌦 ☐ ⛈ ☐ 🌧 ☐ 🌨 ☐

DRAW, SKETCH OR STICK-IN A PICTURE OR KEEPSAKE OF YOUR DAY.

DATE:........................ LOCATION:.. TODAY'S STAR RATING: ☆☆☆☆☆

TRAVELLED BY: ✈ □ 🚢 □ 🛣 □ 🪧 □ 🎈 □
PLANE   BOAT   ROAD   WALK   OTHER

WHERE DID I VISIT?

WHO WAS THERE?

WHAT I DISCOVERED?

WHO DID I MEET?

MY FAVOURITE THING WAS:

MY MOOD WAS 😄 □ 🙂 □ 😐 □ 🙁 □ 😎 □ 😴 □

WEATHER ☀ □ ⛅ □ 🌥 □ ⛈ □ 🌧 □ 🌨 □

PICTURE OF THE DAY

DRAW, SKETCH OR STICK-IN A PICTURE OR KEEPSAKE OF YOUR DAY.

DATE:........................ LOCATION: .... TODAY'S STAR RATING: ☆ ☆ ☆ ☆ ☆

TRAVELLED BY: ✈ ☐ 🚢 ☐ 🛣 ☐ 🪧 ☐ 🎈 ☐
PLANE   BOAT   ROAD   WALK   OTHER

WHERE DID I VISIT?

WHO WAS THERE?

WHAT I DISCOVERED?

WHO DID I MEET?

MY FAVOURITE THING WAS:

MY MOOD WAS 😄 ☐ 🙂 ☐ 😐 ☐ 🙁 ☐ 😎 ☐ 😴 ☐

WEATHER ☀ ☐ ⛅ ☐ 🌥 ☐ ⛈ ☐ 🌧 ☐ 🌨 ☐

PICTURE OF THE DAY

DRAW, SKETCH OR STICK-IN A PICTURE OR KEEPSAKE OF YOUR DAY.

DATE:........................ LOCATION:... TODAY'S STAR RATING: ☆☆☆☆☆

TRAVELLED BY: PLANE ☐ BOAT ☐ ROAD ☐ WALK ☐ OTHER ☐

WHERE DID I VISIT?

WHO WAS THERE?

WHAT I DISCOVERED?

WHO DID I MEET?

MY FAVOURITE THING WAS:

MY MOOD WAS 😄 ☐ 🙂 ☐ 😐 ☐ 🙁 ☐ 😎 ☐ 😴 ☐

WEATHER ☀ ☐ ⛅ ☐ 🌦 ☐ ⛈ ☐ 🌧 ☐ 🌨 ☐

PICTURE OF THE DAY

DRAW, SKETCH OR STICK-IN A PICTURE OR KEEPSAKE OF YOUR DAY.

THE BEST
TRIP

Made in United States
Troutdale, OR
04/15/2024

19200150R00058